sad
thing
angry

Emma Jeremy

Out-Spoken Press
London

Published by Out-Spoken Press,
PO Box 78744
London, N11 9FG

A CIP record for this title is available from the British Library.

First edition published 2023
ISBN: 978-1-7399021-8-6

Typeset in Adobe Caslon
Design by Patricia Ferguson
Printed and bound by Print Resources

Out-Spoken Press is supported using public funding by the National
Lottery through Arts Council England.

Supported using public funding by

**ARTS COUNCIL
ENGLAND**

sad
thing
angry

Contents

sad

the horse could die

how do i make my body fill up again
i was looking out my bedroom window
into a field
where a single horse
was walking in circles
i don't know how it got to this
that horse actually sitting on my chest
its enormous breathing
in my face
both of us filthy
unable to wash in this position
when i try to eat
the horse takes the food from my hands
but it has to eat in order to live
so i can't complain
after all i brought the horse in here
i think it was me that brought the horse in here
and i could have done something else
i could have made the horse
something that didn't shove its living in my face
or made no horse at all
i don't know how to talk about this

wet sand

when i walked into the sea
i didn't think about what i would do
when the water hit my waist and kept going
my bare toes pushing under the wet sand for grip
it wasn't my choice to be here
which implies that choice belongs to someone else
but it doesn't
a bird is still a bird
even when it's under the sea
washing something in water doesn't change what it is
when you take it back out again
dripping wet and sorry
you'll see in the bird's eyes
a bad kind of gratefulness
which you must take
then lie flat on a rock
to dry

all i know is it tumbling out of me

i can only think about us drowning
me — back sitting in that hard chair
spreading my fingers out flat on a table
her — reaching for a glass but not able to pick it up
the fog coming in and the bird at the window
lights off — hoarse breathing
the room full of water but not really
bird looking in at us both
while the room we're in tries to be a room
and so many people not in the room
all talking about dying
using up the words — chewing them
until they don't mean anything
let's talk about how the sea
spits out what it doesn't want
about dogs biting their own skin
when they itch — friend,
passing is what you do
when you're playing a game
not standing in a corridor
the smell of ammonia

it takes many people to prepare

and they do this by piling sticks outside their homes
holding their knees
the less experienced
learn from the others
drink only water
eat things that are easy to swallow
the people who know what they're doing
do the hard bits
the walking in circles
the closing of house windows

when a flock of geese
flies from one place to another
some always get left behind
but a goose knows how to keep normal
in a way a person doesn't
and there's no guidance
no one arrives to explain
that there's nothing to be done
that you'll want something to do
without doing anything
that there's no way to paint your home
in a way that'll make it feel like your home again

so instead the piling up of sticks
the filling up of buckets from the sink tap
the people leaving the sticks outside their houses
taking the buckets of water to the river to empty them
do you see what i'm saying

in the houses there'll be an absence
that fills up every room
everyone will stand up
to make space for it
all of them feeling as though
they're eating all the time
pouring the water in the river doesn't help
the people still holding their knees don't help
what's going on still
goes on

adventure

this is going to be a long one
i am holding onto a pot very tightly
stirring soup to stop it burning
while underneath my hands
in my muscles
i am feeling afraid again
a timer is going down
one stir of the soup takes two seconds
if i really drag it out
i need many of these to fill up a day
you only receive a finite number of choices
and i spend my choices stirring
i take the soup off the heat
pour the soup into a cup
and continue to stir it
until the soup becomes cold
then i pour it back into the saucepan
turn on the heat
and start stirring again
after this long day has finished
i turn the heat off
i turn the light off
and the soup lies in a dark place
until morning

nothing is happening

i am walking through a house
that i recognise from a long time
ago the walls are pink my hands
and my face when i look in the
mirror are pink i am not lying
when i say walking inside is like
peeling off an outer layer of skin
it is cold and the glass on the
windows is frosting no one lives
here not even me which means
there is no feeling of sadness just
nothing as my bare feet walk on
the dark wood floor that no one
is seeing the tables all full of
dried up brittle flowers not in the
shape of a name but in the shape
of nothing i have been here
before but the difference this
time is a safer feeling if nothing
is living nothing can die and
since there is nothing here i am
able to come back again and
again and always find nothing
happening each time i come here
i leave the dead pieces of myself
behind when i come back i can't
find them

the dark dark

when i think about it i see myself as i am
but holding a bucket high up
waiting for anything to drop inside
or holding a door open just in case
i think about the absence of things
not the appearance of them
how the muscles all go soft eventually
how every person will inevitably stop growing
when it comes — the dark dark
i've remembered that i've lived more hours now
than i had yesterday
that speaking doesn't create sense on its own
that the mind works because not working is optionless
that the feet move because what else will take us away
from this earth

sorry

the woodpecker
on the grass outside
the day after
i saw her die
how i watched it
for minutes
hopping around
pecking at the floor
then flying away
leaving me
with nowhere to look
but back inside the house
at my sister
lying on the carpet
to fall asleep
i knew then
that i'd become different
i'd seen my first ghost
and realised
there are no exceptions
now i hold
my hands together under
the tap in the sink
and look outside often
at any patch of grass
for the woodpecker
which climbed into
my life for minutes
then got to leave

lamb

i should have picked up a lamb many years ago
so as it grew into a sheep
i could have grown stronger
you can prepare your body for anything
if you see it coming
most people
like the people i learned from
spend their days not preparing
and when the time comes
to carry the weight of something
large and dense in its difficulty
it can't be done
without your muscles
the bits that keep you together
tearing

reveal

i repeatedly hold an apple to my mouth without biting it
and at the same time think about a woman
standing alone at a sink washing her toothbrush
explaining something is very difficult when you don't exist
e.g. empty packets of tissues mean the end of something
e.g. standing up in a dry bath
can quieten feelings of wrongness
if i leave this door open
it looks like i expect to be followed
and sunflowers actually do mean more than they let on
no one talks about the sea
no one talks about anything at all
especially inside a family home
family homes are exercises in silence
where we all hold hands
the apple means very little when taken out of context

for example

on a hill
a house
inside the house
a smaller house
in which a girl
holds a smaller girl
made of plastic
and moves her hand
up and down
as she looks out
a plastic window
the smaller girl
the plastic one
is put on her side
as if to sleep
while the girl
the flesh and bone one
takes off her shoes
spreads her toes
on the carpet
holds her breath
and imagines
what it's like
to be plastic
to be lying
on your side
in a tiny house
without any
fears or
feeling

no sadness or
enjoyment
to worry you
entirely nothing
no brain at all
to register
anything
to tell you
in your body
there is
something now
missing

two girls

we wake up
walk downstairs
sit together on the floor
one turns on the tv
one pours the dry cereal
into bowls
it's saturday morning
we eat without looking at our hands

many years later
as it always does
something terrible happens
and afterwards we lay in the dark
no bowls
no saturday
just two breathing bodies
living next to each other
each aware for the first time
of the potential
to stop

then waits

there's a plant called
the white mustard plant
that dries out and curls up
when its surrounding
environment
fails to give it
what it needs
the plant then waits
quietly continuing to live
until things are better
only then does it
unfold itself
and become
something again
to be looked at

i talk about the beach

on the beach today it's snowing
and i'm asking now
to be there
my skin dipping in and out of the water
all cold and alive
in a way i don't feel guilty for
at night i'm struggling
staying in my body is difficult
in my dreams i'm under tables
looking up at myself eating dinner
or under my own bed
looking up at myself sleeping
my shoes never on me
and their absence having an important meaning
which is that i'm unable to stand
that i'm always underneath something
looking up or sitting on a ground
which is wet with not snow or sand or salt water
while my real body exists somewhere else
like alongside my friends
sitting around a table
all of them laughing because
nothing's happened to them yet
my body laughing because
without me it can
and when my friends then stand up
to leave the table they're sharing
i know things are beginning to change
and i know this is happening
because i recognise it as the thing i fear

so i watch my friends becoming good fathers
my friends building homes for themselves
my friends sleeping well in large comfortable beds
while i have to climb through
everything that needs to be climbed through
to get back to my body which
as i've said before
should be on that beach

thing

the thing didn't appear or arrive. just became. there were days between the cooling of her body and its becoming. those days were heavy but peaceful. contained air that was easy to breathe in. now, when the thing is with me, which is almost all the time, i'm warm with fear. when the thing isn't with me, i can speak in full sentences, but the guilt is terrible.

i'm in bed under the covers,
building something — a home
which i don't have to leave.
outside, there is everything else.
arguments and sometimes love.
all of it harmful. before the thing
became i was small — not in body
but in nature — and that has not
changed. if i ever show courage to
anyone, i know i'll be evicted back
to the outside. and it's there where
i'm alone and real.

what i know i need to say is pushing against the back of my teeth. but i'm not ready. i close my lips together and don't move them at all. not even to eat. when i'm breathing, sometimes words get out and i can't get them back in. they're insisting to be seen all over my face. they keep pushing, all day, until i fall asleep and leave my face lying in a dark room where no one can see it.

i don't want answers to any big questions. when i think about the thing, which i do whenever i'm awake, i try sitting in a quiet room with a small task to complete. but often, this doesn't work. it gets quiet, and my lungs fill up with water. a horrible croaking sound.

i've got no power and i look like it.
fresh air is supposed to help. i know
going back outside is essential. but
i wouldn't find it hard to stay inside
forever. i put on my coat. i put on
my coat again.

i'm drawing circles on a piece of paper. whenever they overlap i stop for one minute. i set a timer so i remember to start again. i can't recall who told me to do this. but when i'm not doing anything, i think too much about the thing. my lungs don't feel big enough to breathe correctly. and when i'm drawing the circles, they look wrong. the pencil i hold hurts the palm of my hand. i remember her hand. her hand underneath my hand. i start drawing. i stop. i wait. when i'm done i wash my hands in very cold water. and i look out the window, unable to breathe.

i go outside. when i arrive at where i decide to go, there are living people everywhere. eating. drinking. breathing without needing to think about it. the room isn't quiet enough. i move myself to the corner of it. i stay there for almost a day, watching the room and the other people inside it. in turns they arrive. they talk to each other. some of them smile. everything looks dirty.

i'm in a swimming pool. on me are clothes. a dress, coat, hat, scarf. my shoes are made of plastic. the swimming pool knows i'm not meant to be in it. but it seems in need of company and attention. the water is cold like her body the last time i touched it. i'm tall enough here to finally feel safe from drowning.

i walk through a garden. the thing isn't with me, and the perceived threat of its sudden appearance ruins everything.

i'm on a roof looking up at a cloud. the cloud makes me think of the thing. the texture is so dense that if it fell on me i would suffocate. but it doesn't fall. it just hangs in the sky, being enormous. i assume everyone else is looking at it too. but when i look down from the roof at the ground, the people walking there are only looking forwards. heads like little black dots.

in the room filled with people, i watch a wine glass. the hand holding the glass rotating in small circles. the wine moving inside the glass. the people in the area around the glass speaking. eating. drinking. not seeing the glass at all. and then the hand suddenly not moving. the wine beginning to slow down. me realising that, eventually, the wine will stop moving too. and me deciding, very quickly, that i won't be in the room to see it happen. i leave before the wine goes still, which means i'll remember it as persistent. committed to moving even though it knew it would stop.

the thing is not a replacement. i
think this long and difficult summer
is all about understanding that. i say
summer not because it's summer.
but because this time has been
made of long uncomfortable nights
of sleep. and a perception that
everyone except me is laughing
constantly.

i'm thinking about the thing in the swimming pool now. my clothes are heavy with cold water. i'm still tall enough to know i won't drown. which means me, my body, the water and the thing will be together until i get out. i take my hands out of the water and place them on the surface as if to push myself up. but then i don't do anything. i stand completely still with my hands on the surface of the water. i'm waiting for something important to change.

i wasn't ready. the piecing together
of my experience has confirmed it.
the thing has made me feel young
in a bad way.

the circles stop working. i think about the thing even when i'm drawing them. i breathe in more than i breathe out. and when i'm full of air, i breathe out the reserves i've built up in one go. a long breath which leaves me empty.

like a bird building a nest. or
the tide coming back into shore.
i've realised the becoming of the
thing was slow. existing already
but meant to be not seen. and not
seen. until it was.

in my bed, when i first wake up,
i keep thinking about her. the
home i've built is no longer
keeping love outside. so i leave. i
lift the covers up, then fold them
back. and when i'm done, i'm
outside again. and the air is cold.
and i exist.

angry

why not

my stomach is pink
i'll show it to you later
wave my hands in your face
i want violence
it's hard to explain
imagine having to peel an orange
in less than ten seconds
then shoving each part
in your mouth
but you're not hungry
you haven't been hungry for a long time
imagine catching a cat
that's fallen out of a window
no one wanting to take it off you
imagine having to look after that cat
when you've used up your love already
imagine covering your mirrors
so you don't have to watch anything live
being in the shower
your eyes not seeing the tiles
being somewhere not wet
but only half there
even though all of it
did happen
and you're sure it actually did happen
the cat clawing at the door
the cat breaking through the door
still it not happening
but happening somehow all the time

and now you the cat and everything
in the shower soaking wet
your stomach pink
by which i mean
my pink stomach pink
from the hot water
and full of oranges
my hands in your face
please don't laugh

scare

i ask to be less aware of the blood in her body
to forget that cells multiply as she gets older
i know enough now
about how a person is made
don't teach me any more
one day a doctor handed me a tissue sample to hold
a small part of a living person in a cup
i'm trying to say
our skin makes mistakes
that only mean nothing sometimes
and like how a spider crawls up a wall to make a web
makes the web
and then has to wait there for something to happen
every time i leave my home
there's nothing outside
except for living people made of tissue
and blood cells
organs and hair

egg

if i had eaten the egg
then it would be inside me
instead of on this plate
my fork would not be clean
my mouth would have done
something useful
i would already be carrying it
around in my body
realising there is dignity
in swallowing something whole

in this example it's a machine

pumping things in and out
a part of a body
on the other side of a room
when i was young i was very sick
this is an important detail
because i grew up thinking
sickness was only for children
that machines were for growing your body
in ways it hadn't worked out how to do on its own
now i know all bodies are machines
we choose to keep running
this is literal — sorry
but grief about your own body hits you
just like grief about someone else's
it feels the same — quiet like an unbitten nail
then suddenly
even quieter
with a quietness
that lasts a very long time
in childhood
machines must work
because if they don't it's unnatural
at some point this changes
sometime between a girl's kidney
growing wrong
and a woman saying
enough now

am i the pig

rolling in the wet dirt
or the dog on the beach
walking its body into the sea
i think
i am the pig
covered in mud
not the dog
putting itself in the sea
looking back at the shore
being so clean and full
of salt water

later
the dog won't
be swimming
will lie on its side
licking its paw
clean of salt
while i put my face
in the mud
and breathe in
and in
until my mouth
is full

nails

if i hadn't picked up the bag of nails
they wouldn't be spilling now in front of everyone
i wouldn't be picking them up off the floor
my bare hands full of nails
shoving nails into my pockets
dropping them again
nails rolling on the floor
i could go on
walking i mean
the nails could keep falling
i could keep picking them up
my hands getting scratched
whichever time it is they've fallen
on my hands and knees
i could gather them up
do anything to carry them
make any kind of promise
anything at all
i'm still figuring out
how much of this
is within my control

takes place

this image: girl and cake
her eyes looking down, hand around a fork
outside there's snow
in which there's a body
and everyone will know that the girl has seen the body
and can no longer eat
there's a question: who will clean up the body?
another question: how long will it take her to eat the cake?
the girl looks like all girls
sitting up straight even though she's distraught
the image will not change for a long time
but when it does the girl will be in her bedroom
the cake on the pillow
will she ever eat? and of course: where is
the body now? everyone will be able to see on the girl's face
that it's still outside
not seeing the body now
will somehow be worse than the alternative
this isn't difficult to understand
what is difficult is that the girl knows something
she shouldn't know yet
that feeling that she was alive
has suddenly been interrupted
it's still snowing outside
we unfortunately all know
what happens next

thank you for changing everything

actually
hold out your hand
into your palm i will put
the half-eaten apple
the heavy ache
this is how you can help me
i will take from my throat
the thing i am unable to say
you can put it up on the wall
we can look at it
it can go in the river
and we can watch it drown
you can take pictures of the apple
eat the rest of it for me
swallow it into your own throat
whatever you think
best

this time the bird

was down my shirt
i undid my top
as if opening
a screen door — the bird
flew out between the second
and third button
and hit the wall of my bedroom
feathers falling off
its body from the impact
the bird flew in circles
around me again
again swooping hitting
the same wall over and over
each time harder
more determined
a year before this happened
the bird was growing
in a nest somewhere
i was standing on a beach
watching the waves
and their indecisiveness
stepping in and out of the coast
unable to get where they wanted to go
the bird was being nurtured
fed before i knew anything about it
in my bedroom the bird
continued to hit itself
with the wall for hours
it would not die

i took a photo of the bird
developed it years later
and could not see it

in bits

a car speeding in front of me hits a dip in the road and flips
turning like a windmill before landing upside down
a hand just visible on the passenger window
pressed flat — hello
i have spent this year trying to be funny
later i'll tell someone about the car
but add that as it drove past me
i swear i saw a dog climbing through
from the back seat as if to say
i am better than you let me drive
and it's a sort of irony that then
the car is destroyed in the most spectacular way
in this version everyone is fine
the passenger with her hand on the window
is helped out of the car by a bystander
the driver takes longer to get out —
a broken arm — but all things considered
after this i go home
i heat myself some soup
and i'll always remember what i saw
when i eat soup from then on
every time someone offers me something to eat
i might say — not soup please —
and sometimes this gets laughs

then withdrawing

i was told to go to a large space
one of those spaces you can't see the edges of
everyone said it would help
fresh air
no city
no people
instead
wind water fish etc
i didn't go then
because i didn't want to go
but i thought about it
imagined my feet
cold in the water
the sea putting out its hand

i'm trying

today is the day
i finally tell everyone
how watching them get older
is making me sick
this isn't appropriate talk
i know that
all panicking should be done at home
and the truth for me may not be the truth
for everyone else
but my hair is growing
the day is happening right now
and finally
i'm being looked at
i tell them there is no hidden humour in grief
i tell them that the empty feeling isn't emptiness at all
that though yes
it's an absence
it's heavy
like i've eaten the whole earth and all its families
and have then been required
to stand in rooms with other people
who don't feel this feeling
a feeling which is a reflection
of the rooms themselves
being empty of people
who understand how much i'm trying
in every room i'm ever in
to stand still

some things make more sense written down

this is not one of those things
i took a branch from a tree
snapped it clean off like it was mine
i waved it around because i wanted attention
actually inside
i wanted no one to look at me
when there is pain everyone assumes there is sadness
i didn't want any sadness assumed onto me
the branch was flexible
it bent in the wind
when i held it up straight
i pointed it at the sky
nothing pointed back at me
later, the sun went down and i was in darkness
with the tree the branch used to belong to
i put the branch on the ground
at home that night i climbed inside my bed
pulled the covers over my face
and suffered

could be

i was myself then
small inside my shirt
body curled over the bed
she was something else
breathing shallow
under a yellow quilt
and in the garden
through fog
a bird
it came
closer and closer
to the glass door
the fog around it
like a wall
and me — i was breathing
and as i've said before
the room was trying
to be a room
the bird was there
and i was afraid
of what we
the bird and i
knew would happen next
what i haven't said yet
is how much
i'd not believed
in anything
until the bird

was looking at me
and for a minute
the minute before
it happened
i've realised since
i wasn't actually
alone

Notes

Earlier versions of several of these poems appeared in *Safety Behaviour* (Smith|Doorstop, 2019).

Acknowledgements

Thank you to the following publications where a number of these poems, or earlier versions of them, have appeared: *bath magg*, *Field Notes on Survival* (Bad Betty Press, 2020), *Magma*, *The North* and *Poetry Review*. Thank you to Out-Spoken Press for the opportunity to produce this book. To Patricia Ferguson for her guidance throughout the process, and for designing this beautiful cover. And to Will Gee and Arji Manuelpillai whose advice helped shape many of these poems. With love to Kirsty Capes, for everything. To my family. To my friends, Danny, Ryan, Charlie, Matt, and Scott. To Kay. With unending gratitude to Wayne Holloway-Smith, whose belief in me, mentorship and support are the reason this book exists. And with love and gratitude forever to Jamie, for keeping life beautiful.

Other titles by Out-Spoken Press